Leonid Afremov: The ARTIST

Dmitry Afremov

Contents

CHAPTER 1: WE LEAVE FOR ISRAEL 3

CHAPTER 2: WE ARRIVE 13

CHAPTER 3: WE TRY SELLING PAINTINGS...19

CHAPTER 4: WE ARE AT WAR...33

CHAPTER 5: WE SELL PAINTINGS..39

CHAPTER 6: KNOCK KNOCK 47

CHAPTER 7: ENOUGH IS ENOUGH 59

CHAPTER 8: WE LEAVE FOR AMERICA 63

CHAPTER 9: NEW IMPRESSIONS 75

CHAPTER 10: HELLO MEXICO! 85

It's so cold to wake up in a frosty winter morning in Mexico! Only 60 degrees, and without heating it is very cold. It's still dark. The Caribbean Sea is splashing outside the window. Staying in bed, I'm groping for my cellphone – it's my daily routine. The website has not crashed. For some reason it likes to crash at night – it's a mystery to me. This is probably the reason why the entire development department is situated on the other side of the globe. Well, now I can open one eye and check the mailbox. There are a huge number of unanswered e-mails. It's Gera's area... apparently last night he hung out at a nightclub with another pretty Brazilian. He is 26, it's a good age to hang out. A quick glance at the social networks; they are Olga's department, so everything is always in order there because she is a very conscientious girl. I am lying in my bed listening to the house. Every day I hope my wife will oversleep and won't wake the child for school so I can sleep in! But I am not that lucky. They are already downstairs – I can hear the plates rattle, which means I have to get up.

Mom and dad must have already woken up too, their cat wakes them up. He likes to eat about five in the morning. And the food has to be fresh, right out of the can, so you can't leave it in the bowl the evening before. Dad says that he doesn't like cats, but besides the big red cat Max who has lived with us ever since I can remember, my parents also have two adopted cats who are always hungry and waiting for any excuse to get a treat.

Today is a memorable day. Exactly 30 years ago, we decided to leave the Soviet Union. It seems so recent! And at the same time so long ago…

Chapter 1: We Leave for Israel

It was the wonderful year of 1989.

The bell rang and a plump 11-year-old boy ran out of the school gates. Why was he plump? Because my grannies always said to me that I had to eat a lot if I wanted to be strong and smart. And I didn't want to be weak and silly, so I listened to my grannies.

Hooray! It's Saturday! Tomorrow is a day off. I don't have to do my chores, and I may watch TV and race my bicycle. Winter will come soon and then the bike will be put into the barn. My bike is sad and lonely there, but in spring we will meet again. But right now I'm running back home as quickly as possible. On weekends my parents' friends come to see us; they are very interesting people. Sometimes they even give me some presents, which I like very much. It takes me five minutes of fast walking to get home from school. The best way is to go through the park, past the prison, through the Smolensky market and then I am home. There is no ambulance at the gate. That's a very good sign, it means that my younger brother is not feeling as bad as usual. He has got some kind of metabolic problem, the doctors don't know what it is, but every two weeks we have to take him to the hospital and put an I.V. in him. The doctor says that he will grow out of it, but our grandmother sighs, "I wish he would grow up…"

I am running up to the porch of our house. We have a huge house, with four spacious rooms. I don't know anyone with a bigger one. All the walls are decorated with dad's paintings. He is an artist. My mother is an engineer, and my little brother Boris is really small; he is always ill and the doctors cannot help him, or they just don't want to, as my granny says.

    From the hallway, I can hear the loud voice of Alexander Markovich Rudin. He is our good friend. Grandma calls him shlimazl, which means "a poor little creature" in Yiddish. He is always unshaven, not combed, his sweater is inside out and his pants are not always buttoned. My parents call him "old impotent" and laugh. He laughs with them too, although I would be offended by the word "old," even though he is already 38 years old and he is three years older than my parents. I do not know what "impotent" means, it probably is just another way to say old. They say he is very clever. He graduated from Moscow State University with honors, and it is quite difficult for Jews to be accepted into that school. He himself says that it is better to be a shlimazl than a hirutene. What's the difference? After all, the meaning of the words is the same. He explains it to me like this: just imagine that a person is carrying a plate of very hot soup, he is very careful, but suddenly – bang! – something frightens him and the soup spills out onto another person! The person who spilled the soup is a shlimazl, and the one on whom the soup spilt is a hirutene.

    "Inessa Grigoryevna, how long are you going to stay

here?" He always addressed my mom by her full name. "Don't you understand that the Soviet Union will fall apart in a year or two? Sodom and Gomorrah will seem a holiday to you! What's keeping you tied down here? This house? Do not make me laugh, you will have such a fabulous apartment *there* that you could push this hut into a corner of it!

"Look at Boris, every two weeks you call an ambulance. And *there* they can really help him. They have got the best medicine in the world. And what is here? Here it's terrible."

I sit down at the table next to my father. He is painting a new picture. Max the cat is playing with a ray of light that shines through the window. I wonder what they are talking about. He has been coming and arguing with my mom for more than a month. Now my mom will say: "After all, there is an army in Isreal, and I have got two boys, and there are Arabs all around."

"So what?" Rudin objects to her. "At least they will serve in the world's best army! And they will defend their real homeland, not hell knows what! And don't forget about Chernobyl!"

We are told that it is too far away to harm us, but I know the consequences will affect our family; if not today, then ten years from now.

Mom objects. "But we know nothing about Isreal. What awaits us there? What will be there?"

"Inessa Grigoryevna, why do you worry so much? Trust me, it won't be worse. Here we are all strangers, and there, it is our home, our motherland. Here is a letter from a good friend of mine, Sasha Trachtenberg. Look, he is writing that they have given him money for renting an apartment and for electrical appliances. He has already bought a French washing machine and a German TV set! But this is not the point. There, you will be where you belong, among the same Jews as you. You will learn the language, find a job, and most importantly your children will fit in better than here."

"But are you going there yourself, Alexander Markovich?"

"Of course! As soon as I persuade you, we'll leave all together."

Then I noticed that the cat was no longer playing with the sunbeam because the light had shifted to dad's canvas. He put his brush aside, looked sadly at everyone and said, "Well, we should leave. In Israel, it can't get any worse than it already is here."

Hooray! We are leaving for Israel! I don't know where it is but it's probably far away. It doesn't matter. The main thing is that there's a sea and it's warm, and we'll be very happy there. But it is not easy to leave Russia. First we'll need to get an invitation to move to Isreal, then permission to leave from the Soviet authorities; after that we have to send our luggage, buy tickets, say goodbye to our relatives whom we might never see again, and do a lot of other things.

Our house feels like it turns into departure headquarters. Mom and Rudin fill out the paperwork, and dad and I packed everything. In Israel you can find whatever it is you want, so why send eleven wooden boxes with furniture, dishes— even two pianos?!

My grandpa Arkady, my dad's father, said, "There, you will kiss every single nail, so grab everything you can take with you." I wonder why we will need to kiss the nails. We don't kiss them here! Maybe he knows better... a lot of people are packing their things with ours: Rudin Alexander Markovich and my mother's entire family; grandmother Asya, grandfather Grisha, my great-grandmother Khaya, and my mom's sister Sopha, with her husband Lyonya and their infant daughter Alina. As I have already mentioned, we had a big house and a huge six acre lot. So the whole yard is filled with big wooden boxes in which we put things every day and in the evenings we grumble why there is so much stuff.

Every day our Jewish friends come to see us and they tell us how hard life will be there. I don't like such stories. How can it be hard? It is Israel after all! I think they're just afraid of changes, so they come up with all sorts of stories. For example, our friend claim that there won't be work, that the wages will be next to nothing and that it is very hot there. Mom says these are all inventions of the KGB. Dad says nothing, and just smiles like a man who is confident and knows that he will be fine whatever happens.

Our friend Marik Kogan came running. He received a letter from his brother who was a professor, a nuclear physicist, and whose wife had been the chief doctor of a local hospital here. They had been waiting for permission to leave for 15 years. And here is their letter with many photos. Marik says that his brother is well settled. As soon as he arrived he was offered a job in a state office. The work is in the open air and there are a lot of colleagues from the Soviet Union around. He does not tell what kind of work it is, although he was asked about it in three letters. Sasha Rudin says you shouldn't ask him about his work. He worked here at home in a secret factory and probably he works at a similar factory in Israel.

"Well, but at least he could give me a hint, I'm his brother after all. He is a professor and I am an assistant professor. What awaits me there?"

"Don't worry, as a last resort you will be a junior researcher."

"You can't take anything seriously, and I'm scared because science is my whole life. I asked my brother but he keeps silence or writes nonsense."

"And what has he written to you?" Sasha asks.

"He wants me to bring plenty of soap and birch-tree twigs for a bath."

"Hah! This is probably some kind of secret code. Try

solving it. A university professor cannot lack soap!" Sasha laughed.

"But are you sure that soap is sold in Israel?" my mother asks. "Lenya and I have bought 50 bars. For the first time it should be enough. And how is his wife Tsilya?"

"He writes that she found a job similar to which she is qualified. Well, certainly, she is not the chief doctor. Who will entrust a hospital to her? I think she is a department head."

"Or maybe a simple doctor?"

"Don't say that! With her experience? By the way, they live in the same house with your cousin Sveta. And she is a dentist."

"It must be a good house if there are professors, dentists and doctors living there. But you, Marik, shouldn't worry. In a month you yourself will be there, you will see everything."

We are all very envious of Marik because he had already received the documents for departure and bought tickets.

Finally, we've got our documents too. Now we can go to Moscow and buy tickets for the train which goes to Warsaw. From there, we will be taken by the "Jewish Agency" out to Israel.

I like trains. There you can sit quietly by the window and eat chicken, which my grandmothers have put in my basket "so that the boy would not get hungry on the road." There are a lot of things in the basket. I think I have enough food to last for a month and a half. Rudin is coming soon, but he hasn't shown yet. Ah, here he is, running. Seeing him, we think something terrible happened. His pants are torn in two places, he is wearing a dirty quilted jacket over a tattered sweater, and for some reason only half of his face is shaved. A bottle of vodka is sticking out of his pocket and there is a hat with earflaps on his head. I saw this hat at my grandfather's home, he said that it was already 40 years old.

"What's happened to you?" my mom cries.

"Inessa Grigoryevna, this is a decoy. I don't want to attract attention, everyone knows that Jews have money and we are leaving for Israel. Let them think that I am a simple worker."

"Sasha," she calls him, "where have you seen such workers? Please take your decoy into another car. You not only look like a tramp, but you also smell like one."

The decoy worked too well because the police detained him right there at the train station. He was taken to the police station, where vagrants, beggars, and drunks were usually detained. As for us, we went to our relatives' home to wait for the release of Alexander Markovich. After two days Rudin returned. He silently showered, shaved, changed his clothes, and then said that he was ready to buy the tickets.

When my mother asked what happened at the police station, he just waved his hand.

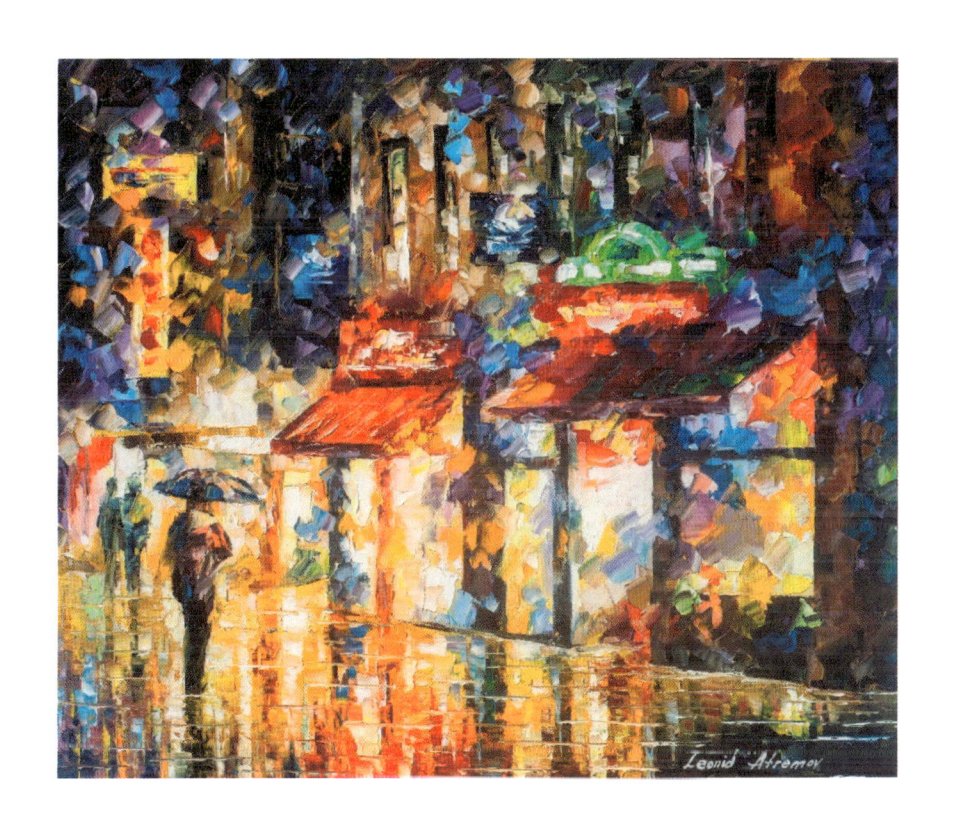

Chapter 2: We Arrive

Do you like to be woken up by birds singing? As for me, I like it very much. But now, I'm wondering why are they screeching so loud? I open my eyes and see three yellow and two green little parrots walking over our suitcases and trunks while Dad is trying to scatter them with a rolled-up newspaper. Ah, I've forgotten to say the most important thing: we made it to Israel!

Let me recount our journey from the beginning. We arrived yesterday, on the 17th of May, 1990. At the airport, we were met by my mother's sister, Sveta Geyshits. We loaded all the heavy stuff into a taxi-bus and drove to the city of Ramat Gan. It's a very beautiful name: "Gardens on the Hills." The apartment rented for us was in the same house where Sveta and our old friend the professor live. They say that the money which the state gives is enough to pay the rent for 6 months. What a generous country! Obviously, therefore, visitors here are not liked very much – Sveta told us this.

But we came anyway. What pleasant smells are all around! They made me feel dizzy. What colors! What shades! And what a bright blue sky! We were all overwhelmed by Israel, everyone in his or her own way. Mom was looking around cautiously. Dad's eyes were like those of a conqueror whose army had not yet approached. Even Boris had stopped crying and was chewing his apple calmly. For me it was love at first sight, and I would beat up anyone who would dare to tell me that this was not the best place on Earth.

Our house looks like a long four-story caterpillar. It's all grey and shabby. Sveta says that it was built under the British, that is a very long time ago. But it is a roof over our heads, what else do immigrants need?

The apartment has a very spacious entrance hall. Straight out of the hall there are doors leading to the bathroom and to the small kitchen. The kitchen is so tiny that Dad said that we would have to take turns to get to the fridge. We are looking for the doors to other rooms but it turns out that this is the whole apartment. Sveta says that the owner promised to put wooden partitions to divide it into several sections. Mom looks like if she has eaten a dead mouse. Dad says it could be worse. Mom replies:

"That is the worst! There isn't room enough for the four of us! What a nightmare! Aren't there any bigger apartments?"

"Of course there are, but you have no money," Sveta answers.

But Boris and I really like it here. At first we wonder why there is no glass in one window. But then we figure that obviously, there needs to be better ventilation. It is said there are no thieves in Israel, so we have nothing to fear.

"It's a pity that Rudin hasn't come with us," says my mother. I think she's in shock, apparently from the flight. When we arrived we parted ways with Rudin when he went to his relatives to the north part of the country.

Here the landlord has come; he is our first Israeli acquaintance. He is of medium height, with a receding hairline and very fussy. At first glance, he looked as though he could be any age, from 30 to 50 years old. If you look at the lower part of the face, it belongs to a young man, but grey hair with a bald spot is more adequate for an elderly person. He brought partitions and divided the room into two parts: one is for our parents and the other is for Boris and me. Then he led our mother to the toilet and began flushing. He didn't speak English and tried to explain us something in Hebrew.

"What does he want?" Mother asked Sveta.

"He is explaining to you how the toilet works."

"Sveta, tell him please that my husband and I have a high education and we did not live in the desert, but in a normal city."

"My dear Inna, it will be a pure waste of time; anyway, we are savages to them."

Finally, the hectic landlord goes away. We could now go to bed. Sveta has dragged several inflatable mattresses, so we will sleep like kings. But for some reason mother is sighing and sobbing all the time.

Sveta promised to come get us the following morning and show us Israel. I count the hours; tomorrow I will see our new homeland.

It's hot. It's very hot outside. I don't understand why

the adults are groaning. I personally like it when it's warm. You needn't spend time dressing, you can put on a T-shirt and run out. Unbelievably, the first person we met in Israel was Itzik Kogan, the brother of our friend Mark, the nuclear professor. He was on his way to his work and part of his area was our street. He was a janitor and every day from 6 a.m. to 4 p.m., he swept the yard and took out garbage.

"At least I work in the open air," he says.

And his wife indeed works at the hospital, but they didn't entrust her to treat people "yet," Marik says, and rolls his eyes to the sky. Now she is supposed to "nikayon." The word means "cleaning" and it's our first word in Hebrew.

"How can that be? You're so smart, so educated! Why are you a janitor?" my mom laments.

"You know, Inna, I am glad to have this job. All of us professors are employed at the municipality, where we have got positions as janitors and watchmen. Trust me, Inna, it is not at all bad because for the local people we are "efes," which means "zero," or "nothing."

Hooray! Here is our second Hebrew word.

"Until you know the language perfectly, you daren't even dream of a good job. They'll pay you peanuts, but you have to be persistent, learn the language and hope that it will be easier for your children."

"And how is your brother getting on?" my mother asks.

"I can't speak about him now." Marik could not hide the tears in his eyes.

During the conversation my father was silent and then asked suddenly, "But is there an art shop where I can buy paints and brushes?"

"Lyonya, who needs your pictures here? Are you crazy?"

"For one thing, I myself need them." Dad replied sharply, and moved away from us.

Chapter 3: We Try Selling Paintings

The first three months in Israel passed like a dream. I went to school; my younger brother Boris attended kindergarten. We studied Hebrew. All of his childhood diseases disappeared, as if they had never existed. After all, a healthy environment and wholesome food matter a great deal. The state paid us to go on excursions. Our family traveled a lot, we visited the whole country. Our apartment began to feel cozy. All the walls are decorated with dad's paintings which he creates every day. "I have never seen such a range of colors, such a palette," he says. He has never seen anything like the colors in Israel. It is a pity that the canvases are expensive. But we have an acquaintance who is a gallery owner, and he has promised that when father paints a sufficient number of pictures, he will organize an exhibition for him. We are waiting for this exhibition more eagerly than a starving person is for food.

Mother got a job as a seamstress at a factory. She starts working at 11 p.m. and finishes at 2 p.m. the next day. When she gets home she sleeps. I wonder how it is possible to sleep that much! So far, it remains to be seen how much she will be paid because it's not common to ask about the salary here.

Today is a joyous day: our relatives from Vitebsk are coming. Mother's sister Sopha is a pretty 28-year-old brunette. Not one is she a talented engineer, she studied Hebrew in Vitebsk. Her husband Lyonya is a photographer and a sportsman. He graduated from the Institute of Physical Education, and he is the only one in our plump family who plays sports. Their daughter Alina is only two and I don't remember her at all. And of course, my grandparents Asya and Grisha and great-grandmother Khaya are coming too. They have already arrived and they are on their way here, in a taxi. Mom literally runs to clean the apartment that she has rented for them. It's over a mile away from our house. The landlady said that only my grandparents and great grandmother could live there. So, Sopha, Lyonya and Alina will crash at our place until they can sign their rental agreement and move to their own apartment.

Hooray! I saw the bus coming from the airport! Outside it was intensely hot, over 100 degrees, but I bounded towards them! Nor was I alone - the whole neighborhood had come out to look at the new immigrants. They were quite the sight! Nobody had ever seen such fur coats and fur caps in Israel! I was never able to explain to our neighbors that it was very cold in Vitebsk at this time of year. My aunt Sopha was the first to get off the bus and she addressed a woman standing next to them in Hebrew:

"Dear Madam, would you please give a glass of water to my daughter? She is very thirsty."

The "Dear Madam" didn't move. She stood agog, gaping at the fur-clad Russian immigrant woman who spoke fluent Hebrew. She had not expected these northern savages to speak such Hebrew.

After tears and hugs we went up to our apartment. My mother came running back from cleaning the apartment. Everyone had a quick snack and then I had the great honor of showing Israel to our relatives. Why me? Because Mother and Father had to take my old great-grandmother to the hospital; she didn't feel very well after the flight, maybe because of the heat.

I was showing Israel as a king shows off his royal realm. I was ready to cut off the head of anyone who would say something negative about my country. But after three supermarkets and two shopping centers, for some reason everyone got tired and wanted to go home.

Today our paintings will be taken to the exhibition. Dad was working for more than a month, and my grandfather and I carried 20 large pictures to the gallery. Meanwhile, my parents were drawing up the contract. My father received 50 percent from each painting sold. The gallery owner priced every piece himself —$1000 for every painting. Of course the contract was in Hebrew, but we signed it. Why would he deceive us? He wouldn't let us come to the exhibition itself. We were told that if the public saw that the artist was an immigrant they might not buy anything. We were sitting on a bench under a lantern and looking at the front door of the gallery. Dad was discussing the Impressionists with Mom. It was their favorite subject.

As for me, I was counting people who entered the exhibition. Our grandparents were there too, and also Sopha with her husband, and of course my brother with our little cousin Alina. The children were busy playing in the mud, the adults were talking, and I was waiting. When the last visitor came out, we went in. All the paintings had sold out! The owner of the gallery shook my father's hand for a long time and said that he had never seen better paintings and that father was a new genius. After that he sent us to his accountant, got into his car and drove away. We got the check for the sale of paintings. It was the first check we receive in Israel. But something was wrong with Dad. Why is he so pale? The check only came to a total of $500. However, everything is according to the law, to the contract. The gallery gets 50% of the profit; from our half, we pay 30% to the seller and 17% on taxes. The remaining money was not even enough to buy new canvases and paints. Father said a lot of things to the accountant and other employees of the gallery, looking them square in the eyes. After letting out a slew of curse words, Dad went away silently.

    In the street we were overtaken by a tall, grey-haired and not very neatly dressed man. He exclaimed, "I left Russia more than 30 years ago and I've started to forget my native language. But I've just heard such juicy cursing that I could not pass by without stopping. Let me introduce myself. My name is Heinrich. I went to your exhibition and I'd like to say that you are a very good artist, but as a businessman you are pretty bad. Who on earth signs such contracts? Don't you know how galleries work?"

"How should I know?" Dad replied, agitated. "I could not imagine that there are such scammers here!"

"Lyonya, it's a very specific business. Let's go to the café, have a coffee. Let's celebrate your first sale and our acquaintance. My treat." When all of us entered the café, I could read in his eyes that Heinrich had not expected so many relatives. Therefore, he immediately announced that they prepared an amazing coffee here, but they had nothing more to serve because it was late.

It turns out that Heinrich worked in the art industry. He owned a frame shop, and made custom frames to order. What a pity that we did not meet him a month ago! But as my grandfather says, better late than never.

"Lyonya, in this world, it's not enough to be only a good artist. Recognition, exhibitions - it's all bullshit! The most important thing is to find sales, not to paint pictures just for yourself. You chose the simplest way to sell by bringing your paintings to the gallery. But in reality a gallery is just a store selling paintings, exactly the same as a grocery store or a shoe shop. Galleries do not even buy their goods; they live off simpletons such as yourself, who deliver them paintings for sale. Imagine you are a gallery owner: you only pay the rent, and suppliers, the artists, bring their goods to you free of charge, and even entreat you to take them. The painter gets only 10-15% of the sale price or even much less, as in your case. The rest is profit. And in fact they have few customers, so today they have doubly swindled you with this exhibition because every client of theirs has bought a picture and you are no longer interesting to them. But the worst thing is that you don't even know what people are saying about your art, why they like it and what doesn't appeal to them.

"But what should I do?" Dad asked.

"There are several ways that you can work this out. I can teach you how to make frames and you can work at my shop. You could also apply for a job as a watchman. But if you want to paint, you'll have to sell your paintings yourself, directly to people. If you want to work with the gallery, then you should always get paid in advance."

The owner of the café started handing out the menu to us. Heinrich noticed it and said that it was high time for him to go home. We agreed that tomorrow he would come around early in the morning and tell us everything he knew about the art industry. We trudged towards home like soldiers who had lost a battle but not the war. Father was very upset that he had no money to buy neither canvases nor stretchers, and even the old brushes were all worn out. When we got to our apartment, Dad pulled out a palette knife with a beautiful lacquered wooden handle from the suitcase. He looked at it and said, "I'll try making a picture with it." He took the last remaining canvas and within 20 minutes he had painted a bouquet of flowers. Then he threw the spatula aside and went to bed.

The next morning started with a knock at the door. There was our new friend Heinrich on the doorstep. He brought with him a big loaf of challah bread because it was Saturday. It turned out that he lived two blocks away from us.

"Now he will be constantly hanging around," Mom grumbled, and went to the kitchen to make breakfast.

"Lyonya, what's this picture? I didn't see it yesterday."

"Oh, last night, when we came home, I sketched it in 20 minutes."

Heinrich squatted near the picture and could not take his eyes from it.

"Lyonya, this is brilliant! So much pain and passion in one canvas, I have never seen anything like that! What colors, what forms, what courage! But I don't recognize the instrument you used to create this. These aren't brush strokes."

"I found this yesterday among our things," Dad said, and showed Heinrich the palette knife.

"Hah, but this is a palette knife. I've never thought that this tool can create such masterpieces! Listen, sell me this picture."

"Why buy it? Take it for nothing," Father said.

"What do you mean, 'for nothing?' Mom shouted from the kitchen. "If our dear guest wants to buy the picture, let him call the price!"

"300 dollars," Heinrich offered.

"Okay, but you cannot pick it up earlier than in a month because the texture is very deep, the paint layer is thick, and it will need to dry for a long time."

"Lyonya, you needn't worry, I'll put it in the trunk of the car and take it away without any problem. By the way, what are you going to call it?"

"Now that I've sold it for 300 dollars, with this money we will be able to pay the rent for a month. Let's say we call the picture 'A Whole Month of Happiness.'"

"No, I don't really like this title."

"Call it 'Blue Flowers.' This title is right for it," Mother said from the kitchen.

"Thank you Heinrich for your purchase and your help, but tell me what to do next."

"First, you will have to paint every day. Second, make something simpler to sell cheaper. I will teach you how to make frames, you can work in my shop and pay only for materials. And as for selling, your son already speaks good Hebrew, make a cardboard box and let him go to frame stores, gift shops, and art galleries and and have them offer to buy your paintings right away. Never leave the paintings for sale and don't give them your phone number. No one will call you back anyway. I believe Dima can do this!"

"Tell me, Heinrich, aren't there honest galleries that want to collaborate with an artist?" My mother asked. "To sign a contract with him and sell his paintings on a permanent basis?"

Leonid Afremov: The ARTIST

"Any contract is voluntary slavery! You sell your skills, soul, and talent for three pennies. They will tell you what to paint, when and how. You'll never know what people think of your works. Their distorted opinion will be transmitted to you by the gallery owner."

"Yes, but when the contract is over, my name will remain," my father said.

Heinrich burst out laughing—"Ha! Your name will remain in your passport. Do you really think that the gallery owner has got many clients? At best, 100-200 people. And when the gallery is closed, you will be forgotten."

"I actually think that art and money are two things which are not compatible with each other," Mom inserted her line into the conversation.

"Oh yes, I forgot. An artist must be hungry!" Heinrich said. "What nonsense! This is the word which I hate—'art.' Nobody knows what it means, but huge money is made off of it. Any dolt is taken—I recently visited an exhibition and saw it for myself. Then a crowd of art critics is invited, media hype is created. And here you are: three brushstrokes on canvas are declared art. And gallery owners sell this 'art' for terrific money."

"Do you really think people do not understand? Do not make people into idiots," Mom inserted again.

"Inna dear, you are naive! For them, it is a party, an opportunity to talk with their own kind, to drink expensive wine and eat good cheese. And those 10 to 20 thousand dollars that they pay for a painting are not big money for them. Many of them hope that the picture will be an investment, but that idea is completely ridiculous. Tomorrow the artist will be out of the gallery and will sell his works for

$50 apiece in the street. And 'voila,' their investment has failed. So what kind of investment is this? Bullshit! In a few years they will forget these art critics, and galleries and the pseudo-artists as well. Art... everything that is made by hands with the soul poured in it is art, and I do not care what art critics say. A picture drawn by a five-year-old child from the heart is much greater art than a tortured portrait painted by a professional artist for money. An artist must create without looking around and especially without listening to advice of art historians, gallery owners and people like me."

"You are talking about the expensive galleries. But where do common people buy pictures?"

"They do not buy paintings at all! The paradox is that sometimes street artists' paintings are considered much better than works exhibited in galleries. But buying on the street is considered almost the same as giving charity. Here I am buying a picture and in this way supporting the artist. But he does not need your goddamn support! It's he who has given you his creation, in which he put his soul, strength and knowledge. And his picture did not get into the gallery not because it is bad, but because he does not want to give it there for nothing and wait until the gallery owner pays him the same money that someone else will pay on the street, or even less. Buying on the street or in a gallery is a matter of geography, not a definition of quality. Sometimes someone will bring me a piece of shit to frame, but they proudly say that it's bought at a certain gallery as if this means that it's already a world masterpiece. And sometimes they bring a painting which is quite an eye catcher and ask me to make a modest frame. I wonder why, because come on, it's a real masterpiece! But they tell me, 'We bought it from a street artist,' and are embarrassed at that.

"Heinrich, it is worth opening our own gallery?"

"Yes, Lyonya, it could be a solution for you. But I hope that one day artists will be able to sell their paintings directly, without intermediaries and exploiters. And then there will be a breakthrough of modern art when people make a choice, focusing on the picture and not on the reviews written by art critics."

Mother came into the room with a bottle of wine which we had brought from Vitebsk and had kept, waiting for the right occasion. Everybody sat down at the table. I was filled with pride at the preparations to sell dad's paintings. It was decided that he would start the following month, when the winter holidays began. Father prepared his works and the box in which I would carry them.

But, unfortunately, we had to postpone this venture until Spring. The pictures were ready, the box too. A new shirt and new pants were bought for the main vendor. But the war began and our idea had to be delayed until victory was ours.

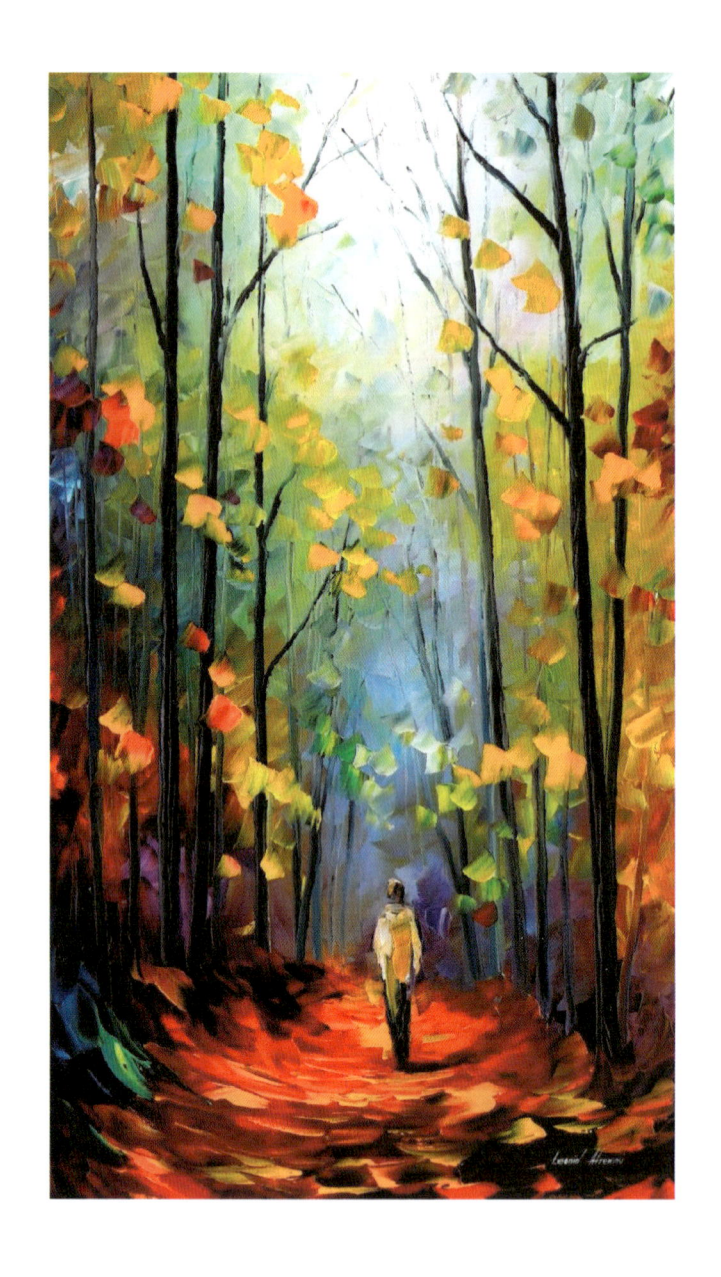

Chapter 4: We Are at War

Today I've come running from school earlier than usual—I have to get gas masks. Dad does not want to go get them; he says it is nonsense and propaganda and nothing will happen. Our army cannot allow some Saddam Hussein to fire at us, to gas us. I believe him, but still it's interesting to look at a gas mask up close. At school, of course, we tried them on, but still I would like my mother to see at home how well I can handle a gas mask. Having stood in a long line, my mother and I received three adult gas masks and a children's one for Boris. On the box written in capital letters was, "DO NOT OPEN!" Dad just smiled and went to paint another picture. The next morning school was canceled. It was so cool! We were told to coat one of the rooms in the house with polyethylene so that in the event of a gas attack the gas could not seep inside. It was decided to glue the bathroom because the window and the door in it were the smallest. It all reminded me of a game of Cowboys and Indians and I enjoyed it immensely. We took canned food and a small supply of water to the bathroom – that's what they had said on TV.

In the evening the TV ordered us to open the gas masks and try them on. Finally! There were so many interesting things in the box: a syringe with atropine, all sorts of powder to treat burns. It was great! The number of our neighbors was gradually diminishing; they were leaving, like rats running from a ship. But we were not going to leave our city! After listening to the news on TV, we went to bed. At night, I was awoken by terrible howling and knocking on the door. Probably, someone hadn't turned off the alarm in the car. But who was knocking at three in the morning? On the threshold, there was a young woman, a native Israeli woman from the apartment opposite ours. She and her husband were newlyweds, but he was a night shift at the bakery, and she was terrified. The woman was dressed only in a gas mask, pajamas, and slippers. She was gesticulating wildly showing us that we should urgently put on our gas masks, and I remembered that this sound means an air-raid alarm; they had run through it with us at school. Dad said, "Well, let's play these games; it must be a training." We slowly took our cat Max and Boris and hid in the bathroom. Then we put on the gas masks and started waiting for something. My brother didn't want to wear his gas mask and was crying all the time. And Dad said, "Inna, leave the child alone. They will sound an all-clear, and we'll go back to bed."

But instead of the all-clear we heard quiet explosions. "It's far away," my mother suggested. At that moment there was an explosion so close that our house swayed like a ship in a storm. Then another one, and another...we felt the house rocking violently; we heard the sound of breaking glass and screeching of stones falling from the ceiling. Mom was cuddling Boris, I was holding the cat. And Dad was saying in a low voice everything he thought about Israel, missiles,

Saddam Hussein and all the rest. But we have agreed that I won't use unprintable words in the book, so let's write that my father was silent. We were sitting and waiting for the gases to flow and wondering how they would affect us. Then another siren sounded, a little different; we all pressed into the walls and waited. At this point, someone knocked at the bathroom door.

"Who is it?" Mom asked.

"It's me, your neighbor," a small voice answered in Hebrew. "All clear, you can come out."

We opened the door. Our neighbor was standing on the threshold. This time she wore only pajamas and slippers, the gas mask was in her hands. We began examining our apartment. The damage was not serious, one window had been broken out, that meant we would sleep with birds. And there were a couple of cracks on the walls.

"They used to be good at building earlier," Dad said.

Do you know what happens after one survives rocket fire? You'll never guess! After the shelling, one is really hungry. The four of us ate our entire week's supply of food. Next morning we went to the shop to replenish our stocks. In all supermarkets there were huge posters: "Foodstuffs are non-refundable, buy wisely." At the same time they accepted everything for payment, even checks without coverage, even receipts promising that "I would pay later." The country united, turning into one big military camp fighting the enemy. On that day, we were no longer penniless immigrants who had come out of nowhere, God knows why. On this particular day we stopped being strangers for the local population because we had not left, but stayed. The war lasted for about a month, with two or three rocket attacks per day.

After the second shelling, we understood that we shouldn't stay in the apartment during an air raid; a missile could hit it at any moment. So we began to descend to the bomb shelter. The main problem was my brother Boris who did not want to wear a gas mask. Mom immediately took off her gas mask too. Dad also removed his gas mask. As for me, I was not allowed to take my gas mask off, but they gave me a lot of advice on what to do and where to go when everyone died. Boris's kindergarten teacher learned that he did not want to put his gas mask. She was nine months pregnant, and yet between attacks she came to our place. She brought a lot of stickers and toys and played with my brother and his gas mask. And you will not believe it—he began to put on his gas mask. And my mother began. And Dad too. Only the cat did not wear a gas mask. Boris suggested putting the cat in a plastic bag in the event of a gas attack. But Max didn't like this idea, he scratched and ran away. It was our routine: there were two or three attacks per night, and during the day everybody went to work. But finally the war was over, and the gases were never used. Our windows got new glass, I returned to school, and my father started painting again.

Chapter 5: We Sell Paintings

I, Dmitry Afremov, am 13 years old now, but still my family won't let me go outside alone. Grandpa Grisha, or "Duta," as little Alina calls him, goes with me. He is 65 years; he is a retired mechanic. He is very joyful and an intense gambler. Every day we buy a lottery ticket – what if we suddenly win? Then there will be no need to sell paintings. But there has been no win so far, probably because adults don't know how to share. So that we do not get lost, Grandma Asya follows us. My mother accompanies her because grandmother is bored alone. On the opposite side of the street, Aunt Sopha's husband Lyonya, in dark glasses and in a sports suit, is strolling discreetly. He is an athlete, a former military man. What if someone tries to steal our money from us when we are running our errands? He will protect us.

"Grishka, do not run so fast, the child will sweat," Grandma grumbles.

"Okay, I'm just checking," Grandpa brushes her off.

Someone has stolen our idea of selling paintings. No matter what office or store we enter, we are told that there have already been five or six artists before us. Grandfather says, "It is good that they've been here, that means it's a good business." And he explains to me that the more they'll say no, the sooner they'll say yes. And so we wander into a large office building where no artists have come to sell their paintings, as the guard told us. However, he looks at us as if we have escaped from a madhouse. Apparently, this is because my mother and grandmother are trying to hide behind the columns. Or perhaps because of Lyonya, who is reading a newspaper upside down. In the building there are some sweet ladies who really love the paintings. We start bargaining; grandfather hisses in my ear, "Stand your ground, don't sell yourself short! If they like the pictures, let them pay." As a result, we sell five paintings, but then the good ladies begin to ask for some receipts. Grandfather whispers in my ear, "Tell them that the receipts are at home, get the money and let's leave!" The women laugh more loudly. They say, "Let's do this: your dad will come here tomorrow and register as a business, then you will come with your grandfather and bring us these paintings. We will buy them from you, and you will give us receipts. There is no other way in Israel; otherwise, we can get a huge fine!"

"But tell me please ,what kind of office is this?" I ask.

"It is the Central Fiscal Authority."

The next day, Dad registers a business and we celebrate our first sale.

I can't say that we make many sales. In reality, our business is going badly. Every day we spend five hours walking and we sell one or two paintings per week. But every Saturday we go to street fairs. I enjoy them very much. We spread out our paintings and wait for customers. After the first sale I am given 10 shekels and I buy myself a pita with shawarma. Once, while wandering through the streets, my grandfather and I came across a gallery. All the paintings are nudes. The owner looks at our pictures, and says that everything is fine, but he sells a very specific product. To which Grandpa replies, "Leonid Afremov is a brilliant artist! He will paint you such a nude that whoa!" What he means by "whoa," my grandfather does not specify.

"Okay, let him paint. Bring it here as soon as it is ready."

After a day and a half dad's painting is complete. It is drying in the sun for a week, attracting attention of the whole neighborhood. Surprisingly, the gallery owner likes it. And he even pays as much as we ask. You see, honest people exist! And he orders 15 more works, but even bigger. We take an advance payment to buy stretchers and paints and dad gets to work. When the pictures are ready, the gallery owner comes to our home to receive the work. I have to interpret.

"Leonid, they are too skinny. Here in Israel men love full-figured women."

"All right, I'll add some weight," Dad says.

"Plus, they are all brunettes. Here blondes are preferred."

"No problem, they will be blondes."

"And the eyes, they must be green."

"Okay, will do."

And so he comes to our place about ten times with different changes and additions until finally he gets what he wants: full-figured women with bright white hair and bright green eyes. Mom always covers these pictures with sheets so as not to embarrass the neighbors who sometimes come to see us.

The day comes that we take the paintings to the gallery. We are surprised to see a large poster on the front door: "For Rent." We start asking everybody where the owner is. What has happened? It turns out that he had problems with the tax inspector and now he is in a place where he certainly doesn't need these paintings. It is a low blow for us. What shall we do with these paintings? We can't exhibit them in a gallery, and they can't stay at home—they take up too much space. But grandfather says that he knows where to sell them. He asks for a little time, adding that all our nudes will fly out of our hands like hot cakes. None of us have faith in grandfather's salesman talent. But suddenly weird characters start coming to our house, dressed all in gold, with expensive jewelry...they look at our nudes, let out approving sounds, pay the requested sum and leave with a painting. Grandfather is as proud as a peacock and says that everything can be sold with the right approach. This continues until one day somebody knocks at our door.

"Israeli police, open up."

My granny goes to open the door. Three men enter the room, two of them wear uniform and one has civilian clothes on. They inspect our apartment with great curiosity and ask:

"What is going on here?"

"Nothing special," I answer. "I am doing my chores, my father is painting and Mother and Granny are cooking. Grandfather is filling out lottery tickets and my little brother is playing with his toys in the corner."

"We are the morality police. Two months ago we made a raid on the hangouts in Tel Aviv. And for some reason, all the arrested mafiosi turned out to have your phone number, even those who are not connected to each other. Your house has already been under surveillance for a month."

And he throws a pack of photos onto the table where one can see people entering our house and coming out with packages in their hands.

"Now you will be searched, but you can hand over weapons, money and drugs in advance."

Father is standing in silence, you can guess why. But here mother comes to the rescue, saying that he is a painter and sells his pictures; he has got a lot of paintings with naked women and these people comes to pick them up. We have a receipt for each sale, where all passport details of these people are written. The police studies the documents very thoroughly.

"Your story passes. But how did they know that you had such pictures? And where did they get your phone number from?"

"They got them from me," Grandfather interjects.

"When the gallery that had ordered these paintings closed, I phoned all the brothels and told them that we had beautiful nude pictures that could suit their interiors—portraits of fleshy blondes with green eyes. The owners were not in and I left our phone number and address with everyone."

"Okay, but how did you find them?"

"Oh, do not make a fool of me! There is a lot of advertising with naked girls on the last page of any newspaper."

"Leonid, tell us how many unsold pictures of such content do you still have?"

"Two pieces."

"Here is our advice to you: close this shop!"

"Why should I? I am an artist, and I have the right to sell what I paint to whomever I want! And I don't need people telling me what to do!"

"We don't tell you what to do. The matter is that two of those men who have bought pictures from you are wanted for serious crimes, and you've got children…"

Finally the police leaves. But one thing is not clear to me: why is everybody scolding my grandfather the whole evening? After all, he has sold the paintings!

Chapter 6: Knock Knock

Two years have passed, and I'm no longer a 13-year-old child but a 15-year-old guy. Now my father and I go sell paintings and the whole family does not follow us. Everyone is sure that nobody will hurt us. Besides, my folks' health has become worse. Our life is like a boxing match without rules, and my mother says that her life resembles imprisonment. She works at the weaving factory 12 hours per day including weekends and holidays. As for us, every day we go around more and more cities in search of new galleries. We did not obey the advice of Heinrich, and daily from 3 to 8 p.m. we get in our car and drive around street after street, city after city in search of success. It feels as though there is not a single gallery or frame store in all of Israel that we haven't been to yet. The most surprising is that everyone likes the pictures, but nobody buys them. Heinrich was mistaken that gallery owners are experts in their field. I think anyone on the street understands a lot more than these so-called professionals. All their knowledge is based on their past sales. A month ago, pictures with red flowers enjoyed success; Lyonya, please add some red flowers to these paintings. Dad is already tired of arguing; he silently changes, adds and does what they ask. Many say, "We saw that customers bought that kind of picture from our competitors, draw us a similar one." Dad figures they don't have the slightest idea of the market, nor of what they sell. We have distributed almost 400 paintings for sale.

To persuade a gallery owner to start working with you is only half the battle; you also have to convince him to hang your picture on the wall in his gallery so that it will at least have a chance to be sold. Otherwise, he will take it to the warehouse, where it will lie until the end of time. Another problem is to persuade him not to raise prices by more than 20 times as to what they pay us. After all, selling a picture for 300-400 dollars is much easier than for 3,000-4,000 dollars. That's why we go around the galleries and check which paintings have been sold and which are still in the warehouse. Sometimes the owners do not even call us in case of a sale, and we only learn about it after two or three months. But we are fighters; nothing can drive us into a corner! While I'm at school, Dad paints without stopping. I do not understand how he manages to find such bright colors in the surrounding gloom. But they are symbolic of our determination and perseverance. We won't give up!

It's Dad's birthday. Usually we don't invite anyone, but today Mother's childhood friends are coming: Boris Pruss and his wife Anya. Boris is a very old friend of mother's; she says that their chamber pots stood nearby in the kindergarten. That may be an interesting way to remember someone, but I have never met a kinder and heartier person. He is very tall, and his weight matches his stature. He has a lush, kind of cavalry, mustache. As soon as he comes into our room, the whole house is filled with good humor and smiles. He works at a factory that produces key chains, in the electroplating shop. Since he is an immigrant, they don't give him gloves, so every day he puts his hands in a vat of acid. You can imagine what they look like.

"Lyonya, your paintings are so beautiful! Maybe I will try selling them."

"Borya, we have traveled all of Israel, and there is not a single dilapidated gallery which we haven't visited."

"But listen, there has come a huge wave of immigration from Russia, almost a million people; in the south of the country, they are building new apartments like crazy. Housing there is not that great, I'll tell you, but affordable. And people need to hang something on the walls."

"You know, Borya, it's not a bad idea. Nothing to lose by trying! It won't be worse than what I'm doing now."

"Because it can't get worse than now," my mom adds.

And here is our first day. Of course you wonder how it is, selling paintings door-to-door. Dad has made a cardboard box on a strap, it fits 10 paintings. We have loaded this box into Borya's old Ford. Mom says this car is older than her. And we set off to the city of Ashkelon. "We" means Borya and me; even though he is much older than I, we are good friends. We stop in the new district. The ground floors are usually occupied by Israelis because there are better apartments. We don't knock on their doors. Starting on the second floor we ring each doorbell, smile sweetly, and say in Russian: "We have come to you with paintings," while Borya is standing behind me, holding the biggest painting in his hands, so that he himself isn't even seen. We sell the first 10 paintings without leaving the first stairwell.

"Good afternoon, we have brought you some paintings." These words start our working day which lasts from three in the afternoon until 10 p.m. There are no days off nor breaks. And sadly Borya and I don't stay together anymore once we enter a building . Now our work looks like this: we drive up to a house, usually a nine-story building. There is no electricity yet, therefore the elevators don't work, but people already live in the house. Light from the flickering candles in the windows can be seen. I start from the top, and Borya from the bottom, and we meet in the middle of the stairs. He is a marvelous salesman. Every day I learn something new from him. Have you ever tried to sell paintings at night without electricity? In the dark they look even better than with light, especially if one puts a candle nearby. The candle light gives such a mystical aspect to the painting.

We decide to take back Father's paintings from all the galleries; that was even more pleasant than a sale, to tell those bloodsuckers that we were not going to collaborate with them anymore. Many did not want to give the paintings back, it turned out they had already got buyers for them. So they had to buy those paintings. It proved to be much easier to talk with the galleries from a position of strength!

After work, at about 11 p.m., Borya and I go to a barbecue bar to have a snack. Borya has a glass of beer and I drink cola. And it's like this almost every day. Today we've visited a 24-story building. There are as many as three elevators. But as you can guess all of them are out of order. Borya is going from the lower floor, and I'm going from the top, after all, I'm the younger one. Somewhere on the 12th floor I ring the bell of an apartment. The door is opened by a man; his face shows that he is suffering a severe hangover.

"What do you... want here?" —and a long burst of juicy Russian profanity follows.

"Good evening! I've brought beautiful paintings to sell."

"Get the fuck out of here!"

"I will, don't worry. But maybe you could let me in and see what I've brought?" (I shouldn't have said that!)

The man gets very nervous, grabs a mop, and I, hiding behind the picture as if behind a shield, run down to the floor below. Here my half of the house is finished. I go to the car, get out a chocolate bar and sit down to wait for Pruss. Twenty minutes later, he runs out of the front door, as if a dog was chasing him.

"Dima, hurry up! Let's get out of here!"

"Borya, what's happened?"

"I knocked at the door of some asshole. And he hit me with a mop, then said he was going call to the police."

Before we leave the yard, we hear the cry of a police siren behind us.

"Oh, gosh!" Borya sighs. "Do you think maybe we can out run them from here?"

"Borya, are you joking? Not in this car!"

A weary policeman approaches us; we both smile at him from ear to ear.

"You were selling paintings there, weren't you?"

"Perhaps," Boris replies.

"If so, you have forgotten the bag with the art, take it away, or they will steal it."

Today we are working in the city of Beersheva. There are new buildings there; people are wealthier and own homes rather than rent apartments. Most of the neighborhoods are single-story buildings. We have to walk more, but the chance to sell paintings is better.

I've got the left side of the street and Borya the right one. I ring at one door and a big dog opens it. I don't know what breed it is, but its head is not much lower than mine.

"Good afternoon," I say. "Would you like to see some paintings?"

"And are your paintings any good?" asks the dog in Russian.

"Very good! You'll like them."

"Well then, come in."

The dog steps aside and I enter the house. There is a man on the floor, he is laying tiles and of course it is he who has just spoken with me and not the dog. That's good to know because I've thought that I am going mad with the heat.

"Don't be afraid of him, he is neutered."

"I am glad to hear that, but to tell you the truth, I was afraid that he might bite."

"No, really! He bites only strangers."

"Then it's a good thing I have family in the area!"

I show the goods to the dog because the man is busy with the tiles and I don't want to disturb him. The dog likes the paintings very much. If he doesn't like a picture, I put it away.

The dog has licked four pictures; I guess the decision to buy has also been made by the dog.

"Your four-legged friend has chosen these paintings for your home."

"Okay, if he has chosen them, let him pay."

"That'll be 800 shekels," I say to the dog. Who knows, maybe he has a wallet too? As Boris Pruss said, "you should never give way to despair: even the most unusual client can pay."

"800 shekels isn't very expensive," the master says, "I'll write you a check."

I take the check, shake the dog's paw, nod to the man and go to our car to wait for Boris.

Time passed, and life ceased to resemble a nightmare from a horror movie. Some furniture started appearing in our apartment; my mother gave up working at the weaving factory; and Dad was painting from dawn to dusk. Our life was getting increasingly bright and light, almost like the same colors in Dad's paintings.

My mother, being the greatest pessimist in the world, warned us:

"Do not rejoice, it won't be always like this."

Father retorted as always:

"Of course, things will keep getting better!"

Now we've been able to open our own gallery, with father's studio on site. This amazing place is located on the first floor of an old shabby building in the industrial zone of the city of Ashdod. We have also great neighbors. On the ground floor, there is a fish shop where they cut fish and sell it to different stores. The temperature outside is over 100 degrees and the stink from the fish is everywhere, but Dad says it is good. He thinks that customers will buy paintings faster and won't waste his time for long. To our left there is a printing house, and to our right there is a billiards club. You certainly wonder why such a great artist as Leonid Afremov opened his gallery in this spot. Firstly, the fish shop clients can come also to us. Secondly, the printing machines in the typography shop emit heat, and during cold Israeli winters we can warm up next to them. And last but not least, is that the rent is very cheap. While Borya and I are running around cities and selling paintings, dad is creating and waiting for customers. Since ours is the only Russian-speaking gallery in the whole city, the chances are good that customers will come because we advertise in Russian newspapers. Today some representatives of a political party have come. We don't really know which party, there are a lot of them in Israel, but they asked Dad to paint a portrait of their leader for free because they don't have money yet, but later, if they win the elections, they will be able to help my father with something. We don't work for free, therefore dad has silently refused. There is a lot of coaxing and bargaining, and finally my dad agrees to paint the portrait from a photo they have left, although he is grimacing all the time.

One of the conditions of the order was that Father himself would hand over the portrait, as a representative of Russian-speaking artists, to their leader. He finishes the portrait and gets ready for the gala. The gala is held at the assembly hall in the city's cultural center, there are a lot of people, the party chairman is sitting at a large table, and behind him there is the flag of Israel. All his henchmen are smiling slyly. And here comes my dad with the portrait. Judging by the face, he has a toothache and indigestion at the same time. The chairman says:

"Thank you, Leonid! I am touched. Now you will go down in history as the person who painted my portrait."

"And I believe that people will only remember you because I have painted your portrait."

And with that Father turns around and heads for the

exit.

Chapter 7: Enough is Enough

My mother, as always, proved to be right. Selling door-to-door is getting more and more difficult. There is no more new construction, and those who moved here five or six years ago have already bought from us ten times. But Borya and I don't give up! Day by day we go around the neighborhoods inhabited by people from the former Soviet Union with bags of paintings on our backs. Many people already know us, sometimes they even give us advice shouting, "Someone new has moved into that house, talk to them!" That is how we live.

Tomorrow I have to go to the Military Recruiting Office. I have already been there three times, answered a lot of questions, passed various exams, and now they want something from me again. I come with Borya Pruss to the recruiting office. I thought the whole thing wouldn't take me more than an hour and a half and then we could go sell pictures as usual. But today I'm surprised by the huge number of people at the recruiting office; many young men have come with their parents or girlfriends, and now they are sitting, tense, waiting for something. Well, this is definitely not my concern. Today we are hitting up a new nine-story apartment building—such a chance is rare nowadays. Here I am called and I say: "Borya, I'll be back in half an hour and we'll go." I return in an hour with a military uniform on.

"Borya, just imagine, they've given me a uniform. Now thanks to it we'll be able to sell more pictures."

"Dima, hey, they've given you the uniform for free and now you may leave?"

"Well, nobody asked for money," I grinned.

"And when do you have to go to the army?"

"I don't know, maybe in half a year, maybe earlier; I haven't asked and they didn't tell me."

I hear my name through the loudspeakers. I'm urgently called. Maybe I forgot to sign something, or they will take away the uniform. I am ordered to get on a bus. I object, "Why the bus? I have a car nearby! And will it be a long drive?" "No, not so long," they answer, smiling. Okay, I'll go by bus, why not? I've got some free time. It is just not clear why everyone around is sad or merry. Other recruits are embracing their parents and girlfriends. I don't think about it because the nine-story apartment building is waiting for me. I put earphones into my ears and wait for the bus to take us to our destination. The journey doesn't take much time—about three hours. My mood is nasty: Borya has gone to work the nine-story building alone. We agreed that when he finished, he would come to pick me up. And here we are. There is a desert and a lot of tents around. Some people with epaulets shout at us and make us line up. I come up to one of them and say:

"Dear sir, I've already seen everything. When can I go home?"

He looks at me with a gaze that psychiatrists probably

use when looking at their patients.

"Home? The first leave will be in about three months."

"Did I get you right? Three months? Does that mean I got drafted?"

"You got me right, Soldier, fall in!"

I sigh deeply: now I'll never get a chance to sell paintings at the nine-story building. I take out my mobile phone, dial Mother and say:

"Mom, you won't believe it…"

"What's not to believe? Are the pictures stolen?"

"No…"

"Is there no light in the nine-story building"

"No, Mom, I've been drafted into the army and they say I will be home in three months."

Chapter 8: We Leave for America

Five years have passed, and here I am, returning home with a bag over my shoulder, this time for good. What happened in the army will remain there. It had no effect on the work of Leonid Afremov, therefore I will not talk about it. A laid table is waiting for me at home, and there is a guest. It is Alexander Markovich Rudin. He and my mother are arguing fiercely.

"Inna, how long are you going to be stuck here? Lyonya's gallery is hardly alive. You work 12 hours a day. And your husband is a brilliant artist, even an American journalist, having visited his exhibition, wrote a whole article about it."

"Well, actually in the article he wrote that Lyonya had not only beautiful pictures, but also a nasty character."

"So what? He is not paid for his character. We forgive the genius a lot of things... And think about your younger son Boris! He will go to the army in a couple of years. Do you want to stay up at night again?"

"Sasha! And what about you?"

"Well, I'm doing great. I've applied for permission to move to New Zealand and have already obtained it. I leave in a month."

"But why do you think that you'll feel better in New Zealand than here?"

-"At least there we won't be constantly bombarded with Syrian mortars. You know, I live in the north, and I'm already fed up with the constant shelling from Lebanon."

"Well, I don't even know what to tell you, Sasha. It's not that easy just to pick up and leave."

Dad smiles sadly and says:

"Well, why not? Let's go! Dima is already free; I've got a sister in New York. Why not try it? Life is too short to be wasted."

At this point, someone knocked at the door. There stood an old acquaintance, a gallery owner, on the threshold. He had been selling Dad's paintings for several years, paying a penny and sucking the soul out of us. He didn't know anything about art but he wore a bright blue beret and a yellow scarf. He had read somewhere that a true artist should look that way.

"Lyonya," he shouted from the doorway, "I've got terrific news! I've found a buyer for your three paintings." Dad's face twisted, as if they had extracted him a tooth without anesthesia.

"Which ones?"

"You see, most clients don't like your pictures because of their excessive brightness. But the design of another painter's works suits them well."

"Then why have you come to me? Go find the other painter."

"He wants a lot of money, and you could make copies

of his pictures, and I would give you $100 apiece, - and he threw several large color photographs on the table."

Dad took them squeamishly in his hands, looked at them, and threw back.

"There is neither color nor composition here."

"You see, it's half an hour's work for such a master as you."

"Do you really think I create my paintings for a miserable 100 dollars? I am looking for the color, a pure, real, vibrant color."

"What's this about a color? What do you mean?"

"What, didn't you go to school. Are you a gallery owner and yet not acquainted with art history? Well here, I'll teach you a lesson."

With these words, Dad got some green paint on the palette knife and spread it over a canvas.

"What do you see?"

"A green color."

"That's right," father said, "a dead green color, the same as on these photos. Now look here," and he put two strokes on the canvas— one yellow, the other blue. "Take two steps back," he asked the gallery owner. "What do you see now?

"Also green," the gallery owner said, grinning.

"This is called Impressionism. It is not a mechanical, but optical color mixing, just like on a TV screen. The emergence of Impressionism was predetermined by invention of photography in the middle of the 19th century. It was no longer necessary to capture the faces of people and the surrounding reality as they were. The camera and the movie camera, which appeared at the end of the century, did this job in the best way possible.

"The essence of Impressionism is live painting 'en plein air,' that is, in the open air. And during this same time another invention arrived—the appearance of lead tubes with paints. Prior to that, the artists had to purchase powdered pigments and oils, which they had to grind and mix themselves; so it was extremely difficult to take prepared paints out of the studios and to work outside. Of course, the Impressionists painted many series of studies of a single object. This is what Claude Monet did, for example: he used to put a dozen of canvases near a haystack and, when the sunset began, worked on each of the canvases for five minutes because the lighting was constantly changing. Thus, he painted ten pictures, in each of which the stack turned out to be lit differently. It's certainly interesting, but it has value only in purely technical terms. Nevertheless, all of the greatest masterpieces of Impressionism were made in the workshops. For example, I've visited the Van Gogh Museum in Amsterdam, and the whole museum is hung with his paintings, but the most impressive thing there is one small drawing that he created at the very beginning of his artistic work. It can be said that this piece in black and white preceded the whole explosion of colors and light. It's called 'Potato Eaters.' It is rather small, but there are always crowds of people around it. This is a masterpiece that makes a great impression, and after having seen it you can no longer look the rest of the museum with any interest.

"I don't paint from life because real nature, when you look at it, holds you and does not let your imagination go free. It is impossible to come up with anything, here is the thing that you are painting and that's it. And you are trying portraying the subject as good as you can. But I want to work from the inside, to show what I have in my soul, so that it would not be about my impression of what I've seen, but about the viewer's impression of what I've felt. I was preparing for such work long before today. At the time when I was at school, then at the art institute, I always had a notebook and a pen filled with black ink on me, and I used them to make sketches. Why wasn't it a pencil but a pen? Because a stroke made with ink is impossible to correct. I had to make precise strokes and accurate sketches on the spot. This imposes discipline. And it helps me now in my work. Because when I paint my pictures, it's good if I manage to finish everything in one session, and if the picture is large, with a complex plot, then I mentally break it into several parts and finish each part in one session. To do this I need to constantly keep the whole composition in my head.

"Why should I convey the state of nature or objects most closely to the original? Any schoolchild with a digital camera can do it better! Today the task of painting is critically different —to transmit the feeling that you are experiencing. If I hear some music, I want my canvas to reproduce the same music. And I do my best to make the spectator of my painting feel the same what I have felt. And the narrative is not so important, more important is the combination of colors, the mosaic of brush strokes. While visiting European museums, I understood that talented abstraction can be much higher and more interesting than so-called "realistic" art. So far, I have not seen a better abstract artist than Pablo Picasso: his paintings are really brilliant, and the less figurative they are, the better they are, the stronger they affect the viewer. I deliberately go to museums because I believe that a reproduction of the picture or its computer image do not produce the desired impression. Each painting contains the artist's energy, and only standing in front of the original you can feel and comprehend what is happening there and what the artist felt.

"Modern painting tends to become equal to music. After all, what is music? It is non-objective: we are affected only by sounds, all kinds of sounds that do not represent anything. Under their influence, we imagine various plots. And such is the abstract painting. I would love to be an abstractionist, but unfortunately it's not for everybody. To express my feelings I need to portray an object, I am not capable of abstraction. Actually, such artists are very few in number. For example, Picasso was capable, but Chagall was not, although they are both equally brilliant. I have a greatest respect for both of them; they are the best painters of the 20th century.

"Here color comes to the forefront of painting. With the help of various color strokes, their vibrations, their ratios, one can convey feeling and mood, a viewer can even hear some music within him or herself. I have pictures that are musical not only in essence, but also in content. I enjoy depicting an orchestra, musicians, but in order to be bound neither to a certain orchestra, nor to a musician, I depict them in the form of cats. This is a cats' concert, as I call it; I've got many such pictures: cats that are dancing, cats that are playing musical instruments; and here nothing holds me back. After all, if you write a science fiction novel, no one will tell you that everything was otherwise, not as you've described it. It's you who have invented it all! The same is here: I myself invent everything and convey my mood through these pictures, that's all.

"I began my first experiments with a palette knife when I was a student, and after that I periodically returned to this tool, but it never occurred to me that I could paint a whole picture with it. I started painting using solely the palette knife only on my arrival in Israel. Here in Israel there is such sunlight, such colors around, and together they affected me in such a way that my brush could no longer cope, because I wanted to make pictures brighter, brighter and brighter. No matter how thoroughly I washed the brush there always remained the previous paint on it; but the palette knife can be wiped clean and each stroke is a pure color, not spoiled with another one. As a pictorial tool, the palette knife has many advantages, but there are also many difficulties. For example, if the paint layer has dried up, even a little, then it is impossible to continue the work. The piece that you paint with a palette knife must be finished in one session, within one day, you cannot return to it next day. Of course, it is difficult, but I have already said how I prepared myself for this; in general, if you keep the whole picture in your head, then it's okay, it's simple.

"Classical art method teaches that you have to work on a picture layer by layer, first elaborating the light and shadows, gradually strengthening them, that is, you have to develop your picture like earlier a photo in the bath with the developer. In order to paint with a palette knife, one has to break completely this method, to do everything in an entirely different way, depending on one's artistic experience, to the extent to which one is capable to do it. In any case, so far I have not met a single painter who would work exclusively with a palette knife and only with it: all use it simply as an auxiliary tool.

"Now I'd like to talk about painting in general. The modern school of painting is slowly declining. Of course, it still exists in some places, such as in Russia. But in Europe, in America, what is taught to children, what is taught to students? It is unimaginable! Still, there are artists who are worth something, artists who, so to speak, are able to paint, but their works, just like mine, are inexpensive, are not sold for millions; art galleries are not interested in them. Instead, all kinds of "magicians" are cheered on, who don't really know how to draw, they can only show off concepts. For example, I myself had to see this in New York, in a gallery in SoHo. It's a prestigious place: there are the best galleries and the best paintings for sale. One of the galleries was covered with wooden slats up to the ceiling and around. I asked,

'What is this? Timber for sale?'

'No, it's an installation.'

'Well, what's in it? What is it?'

"In the same city, New York, in the Metropolitan Museum of Art, they exhibit pictures of the traditional old masters, but also display paintings that are gifted to the museum. Everyone presented something to the museum, therefore the level of artistry is not very high, far from that of the Hermitage.

"In some American art museums you can see such a thing, for example, as a vintage printer with a bunch of paper cascading out of it; this is called an installation. Or there is a toilet, or something else like that. Do you call these works of art? It makes me spit! That's for sure, from the top all the paths lead down, it is difficult to imagine such degradation. I daren't even think what will happen next! And near that, there are normal artists who paint their pictures from the heart, which are nice to see, but they are hardly appreciated. Only now, with the help of the Internet, all these artists have the opportunity to find buyers. After all, in the end, the spectators in the theatre vote with their feet. And how does the painting viewer vote? He votes with his wallet: he gives the artist the most precious thing he has—his money, and if he does so, it means that he sees value in it. A picture cannot cost millions, a now living artist cannot sell his pictures for millions; this does not happen, these are fakes. Several thousand dollars, even tens of thousands - this is the normal price for a painting, for a good original. But then the artist must receive all this sum of money and the gallery owner cannot stand as a barrier between him and the consumer."

"Okay, okay. Just don't get excited. I'll give you $ 150 for a picture, deal?

"Ran, you know, we've decided to go to America and I want to tell you what I should have said a long time ago: 'Go to hell!'"

"Inna, talk some sense into your husband! You'll starve there. Who needs you there? I can understand, he is an artist and all artists are crazy, but you are a smart woman

—$ 450 is a lot of money!"

"You know Ran," my mother said, "we are not needed here either, so go where you were sent!"

"You will live to regret it bitterly! You will offer me your pictures for $50 apiece, but I won't take them!"

Father turned away intentionally. The door slammed behind him, the gallery owner was running down the stairs, taking with him our resentments and humiliations of the recent years.

Chapter 9: New Impressions

It's raining heavily outside. Father is rushing to paint the Brooklyn Bridge. Boris and I are going to help him: I'll hold an umbrella over my father, and my brother, over the easel. It's already the third picture of this bridge. Dad tries conveying the rain as it is. I suggested taking a good photo, but he refused. He says in order to paint the rain, you have to feel it. We are now in America. We are freezing in Brooklyn, waiting for emigration papers. Meanwhile we stay in the apartment of my father's sister, Innochka Baranova. They were happy to have us in their home. They've got a big apartment, two rooms! The lawyer promises that our documents will come any day now. And then we'll leave for sunny Florida. In the meantime, I sell paintings in galleries, Mom helps with household chores, and my brother carries Dad's easel after him through New York City streets, where Dad paints more and more pictures nonstop. What can I tell you about American galleries? They are not much different from Israeli ones: people speak English in them, all the rest is the same.

 Finally, the painting is finished. Judging by father's face, he is not very satisfied, or he is cold, or both. He tries combining the Israeli sun and the New York rain in one picture: a glowing rain. He works a lot—we hardly have enough time to bring him canvas and paints. Now it's time to grab a taxi and go home. But at this moment father just stands there rooted to the spot: his sister Inna gets off the bus, opens an umbrella and comes running towards us.

"That's it!" Dad shouts, "Stay where you are!"

In a minute he sets up his easel, pulls out a small canvas and in another 10 minutes the painting is ready; and this time it's exactly what he wanted: rain and joy together on the same canvas. He will call this picture "The Princess of the Rain." He returns home a winner: he has won the rain, and now he can move on. Many say that rain is gloom, but in father's paintings rain is a holiday!

It's finally warm: for a whole week we have been living in Fort Lauderdale, Florida. This is a good place: there are many galleries here, so I have something to do. Father is finishing the New York series, and my brother and I are going round from Orlando to Kivest, offering dad's paintings. Today we've got an order. An American acquaintance of ours wants father to paint a series of ten pictures on which there will be only bottles, but the main thing is that they must be alive. He was not able to explain what "alive bottles" means: should they have legs and arms or should they look like normal bottles? Father liked the idea. But where can we get the bottles? We do not drink alcohol, and just to buy and pour makes no sense. And then my brother suggested buying empty bottles on eBay. Finally we receive a box full of wine bottles, bottles of whiskey, some of them seem to me perfume bottles. But it's not enough for dad. He takes a camera, and we go to jazz clubs, he photographs jazz musicians, their faces and the way they move. And the series "Bottle Jazz" is ready. He has managed to combine the rain, jazz, bottles, the sun, and light in one painting. When our acquaintance comes to take the paintings, he shakes hands warmly, asking my father:

"Leonid, why don't you sell your paintings on eBay?"

"Is it possible?"

"Of course, it's very easy. Take a photo of your painting, give it a beautiful name, write a description, open an eBay account and auction it off."

"And what price shall I set?"

"eBay is an auction. Set the initial rate of $100, and then let the people bargain."

"And what about money? Will I get it out of the disk drive?" Dad asked.

"No, of course not. You'll set up an account with the PayPal system and your customers will pay through it; after paying a small commission you get the money directly on your bank account."

"And do people really trust this?" I asked.

"Of course, because if something goes wrong, PayPal will take the money from you and give it back to the customers."

"Okay, why not?"

Twenty minutes later, our shop on eBay was open and we placed the first painting there. It seemed some kind of computer game. But why not try? The auction lasted for a week, we completely forgot about it... And just imagine my surprise when I got a letter writing that the painting had been sold and paid for! The small picture went for 300 dollars.

"Let's put everything that we have on there," Father said.

Since then, the era of eBay began: customers bought everything that my father painted; I did not have enough time to respond to letters, nor my brother to pack the pictures. I had never seen my dad so happy; he was not particularly worried about money - for the first time in his life, he had the opportunity to communicate with buyers directly, without intermediaries. That is very important for an artist.

"It will not always be like this," my mother used to say. And one day our shop on the eBay was suddenly closed. If lightning struck our house we would not have had such a shock.

"How could they do this? Why? After all, we pay them crazy money every month," Father said.

"Their letter says that we have violated some of their rules, and they will open us only in a week."

"But which rules? What have we done wrong?"

"I don't know, I'll write them a letter, maybe they will answer."

It was one of the longest weeks of our lives. Dad experienced heart pains and we became acquainted with American medicine, which turned out to be quite good, though rather expensive. Exactly a week later, our shop was opened again. Things went back to the way they had been before, but the feelings of lightness and confidence disappeared somewhere. After all, if they closed us once, they can do it the second time. Every new letter from eBay seemed a letter of closure. So one day I decided to create our own website on which we would sell dad's paintings autonomously. Father got better, and now he is working on the order of one very rich client: a portrait of four puppies. The order was issued through eBay, but there was one special condition: for each correction, he would pay an extra $100. At first the corrections were funny: the dog has 20 whiskers on the photo, and only 19 in the painting. Dad had to add one more. Then there were not enough bells on the collar, etc. There were more than 15 changes in total. The client finally received the painting and was very pleased with it. He placed another order, this time for a portrait of his wife. Dad said: "Well, now the changes will be endless. The wife is quite another matter, she is not like dogs." And guess what? The client, not even looking at the portrait, immediately approved it—probably, the puppies were more important to him.

Oh, what a headache! I have not left the computer for

12 hours. I am making a new site. For a person who understands very little about programming, this is a great achievement. A hot Florida wind is blowing through the window and shaking the blinds. My whole table is buried in pizza scraps and something else that has evolved into a new life. Everyone says that I am mucking around: on eBay clients buy pictures willingly. Why do I need a site when everything is fine? Obviously, I am quite like my mother: I know it will not always be like this. I hear sounds of jazz coming from dad's studio: he also has not got up from his easel for 12 hours because he wants to breathe jazz music into his canvases. His art is like jazz, it reminds him of syncope, there are the same torn strokes from which the whole composition is created. He is working so enthusiastically that he doesn't notice anything around. Just a little more time and the painting will sing, but meanwhile he is the one singing. It's good that we live in a remote area, otherwise the neighbors would definitely call the police. It's already 1 a.m. I enter the workshop, my eardrums are beaten by basses, and Louis Armstrong is singing "What a Wonderful World." I am 100 percent sure that my dad is painting a portrait of a jazz musician. I look over his shoulder and see a landscape: the sun, rain, a couple under an umbrella, a lake and a lot of trees. Father turns off the music, but the painting keeps playing and singing in my head. Dad stretches wearily, kicks the cat sprawled under the

easel and says:

"Tomorrow we'll place it on the eBay. How will we call it?"

"I think "Alley by the Lake."

"Isn't that too plain?"

"I like it. And keywords in the title are good: 'alley,' 'lake.'"

"Do you really think that someone who is looking for a lake or an alley will buy this painting?"

"Today, maybe not, but who knows what will happen tomorrow?"

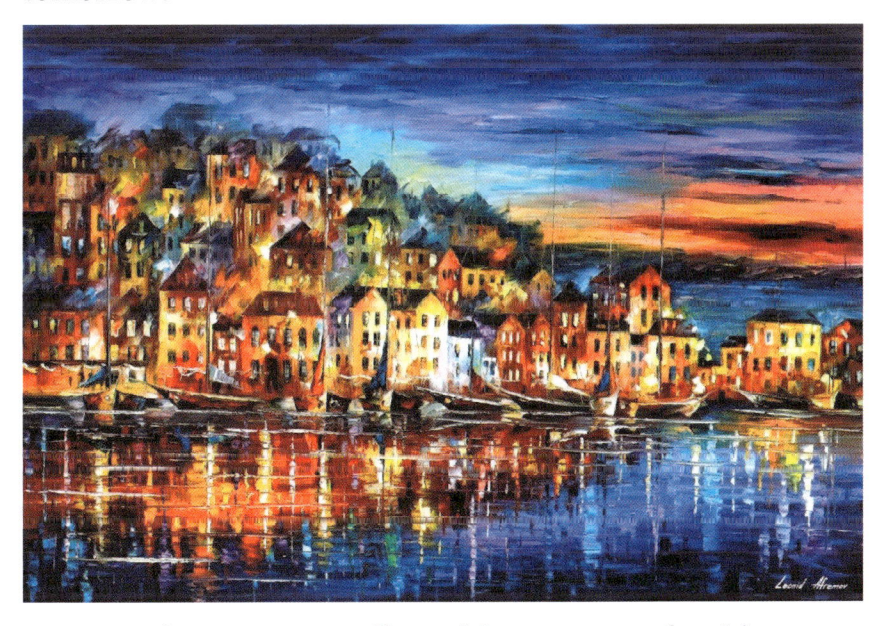

We've got a small problem, or maybe it's not a problem. Dad does not have enough time to paint as many pictures as people want to buy. What to do? An interesting idea occurred to me: why not make reproductions? Once I visited an exhibition and saw a large printer printing paintings, the artist added two or three strokes, then all this got varnished and was called a "giclee." "Why not try?" says Dad. The printer itself is inexpensive, but the main problem is with photos. To take good pictures, you need a camera which costs several tens of thousands of dollars. So we use a normal camera that belonged to Dad. Of course, our reproductions lack sharpness, but dad made up for it with the number of brushstrokes he added to the print. Funnily enough, our giclees were not at all in demand on eBay. Instead something happened that I couldn't even imagine: all the galleries and wholesale stores to which I had offered paintings earlier began ordering our giclees in such quantities that now we've got two printers going and dad has the best digital camera. I still cannot understand this paradox. Why do stores and galleries take reproductions, but refuse the originals?

Today is a special day, my website is finally ready. It took me almost two years of hard work. Probably, if I were a real programmer, I would have done it in three months. But now I know everything about making websites. "Well, let's see what will win: my website or eBay?"

eBay proved to be the winner. Nobody went to my site, except for Mom, but she was there regularly. We need to advertise. I was a complete novice in electronic advertising, just as before when creating the website. That's why we posted our first advertisement on Russian television in New York. By that time my brother Boris was finishing his studies at the college with a major in Cinematography. He made a cool commercial and that was our first advertisement. Obviously, I am a bad programmer, because the site crashed the first minute the ad was shown on TV. I did not take into account the number of visits. Well, that's all right, I'll learn from my mistakes—next time it will be better. However, people still seemed eager to buy Father's paintings, because sales were being made on the site, which was half frozen.

Chapter 10: Hello Mexico!

While taking on eBay and website developing all of us—Mom, Dad, Boris, my little daughter Michelle and myself—live under the same roof in the city of Boca Raton. We live quite comfortably but, Dad wants to have his own place, preferably by the sea, in a new house in a private area. We are in America, the land of unlimited possibilities. Surely something will come up?

A Russian realtor works with us, a tall, thin, eccentric 60-year-old woman; she has been living in America for 40 years and has had four husbands during this time. Right now she is divorcing her current husband who is 20 years younger than her. Her sharp and loud voice works its way through father's speakers even from outside. Dad doesn't like her very much, but she made friends with our mother.

"Innochka, here you cannot buy anything for your pennies."

"Well, I don't know, we could ask for a bank loan."

"By the time you have it, I'll grow old."

"Is it possible to get older?" Dad grumbles from the next room.

"I need to receive a commission as soon as possible. I've been stuck with you for two months! And I've found a wonderful option for you: two houses by the sea. The price will suit you, you'll even have money left over. My friend, the developer, will take you there on his plane."

"Stop, Laura, what plane? We need a house nearby."

"Oh, don't bother my head! It's a little bit south of here, by the Caribbean!"

"Oh, that's probably Kivest," I said. "I love Kivest!"

"You see, Dima already likes it. We are flying out tomorrow; just don't forget your passports."

"But why do we need passports?"

"Well, you're going by plane."

"Okay, let's fly then."

At the Fort Lauderdale airport we were awaited by a little Cessna. We enjoyed the flight: champagne, caviar and Laura'a stories about her life, men, and how many houses she had already sold in that city. Even the biggest headphones didn't save Dad from her voice, so he just pretended he was asleep. We land.

"Now we'll go through Customs, and then there's another hour of driving to get to the houses."

"Laura, where have you brought us? What customs?"

"Oh, I forgot to tell you, we're in Mexico. And the plane won't return till tomorrow."

I am not going to reproduce father's words here, let's say he remained silent.

Mexico. If Laura had not said it, we would not have guessed. The same cars, same roads and same palm trees. The city where we arrived was called Playa del Carmen, and the houses there were indeed such as Laura had described to us: right on the shore of an incredibly blue sea. And the price was right. In the evening, a family council was held over glasses of piña colada.

"Well, what do you say, are we moving to Mexico?"

"Lyonya, what Mexico? We have a business in the USA!"

"Mom, the business can work even without us, everything is well organized there."

"But what shall we do with the eBay? How will they take the fact that we'll be sending pictures from Mexico? They'll dislike something and close us again."

"Why does it matter for them where we are located? The important thing is *what* people get, not from where!" Father exclaimed.

"And let them close us," I replied. "A month ago they changed something at eBay and sales dropped significantly, not only ours, but of all the artists. You know, I communicate with many of them. Therefore, people who are looking for Dad's paintings find them on our website."

"And what does Boris say?"

"I am enjoying myself here: there is so much music, many girls, it's a real holiday! You can go back home, and I'll stay for another week."

"And why can't we have three houses: a small one in Florida and two large houses in Mexico? Look for Laura, tell her that we'll buy them!" Dad ended the discussion.

"Wait, wait! How are things going on here with taxes,

with life? We know nothing about Mexico."

"Let Dima clear up these things, it's his department. And for me the most important is to have the possibility to see the sea from my studio. Just imagine what seascapes I can paint here! Right now I would sit down and create a painting!"

"So...what's the problem? Let's go buy paint and canvases, that way we'll know how much they cost in Mexico."

We found a taxi driver who took us to an art store. And an hour later, my father had an easel, paints and a stretched canvas. All the Mexicans we met spoke English. And our credit cards were accepted without a problem. We still had six hours until the return flight home. Dad went out to the balcony and in just an hour and a half painted an amazing seascape. I began thinking about the name, but he said that this picture already had a title: "Touching the Horizon."

People compare fast things to the speed of light. But it seems to me that time flies faster. We have been living in Mexico for eight years now. My brother Boris has met his love here, and I've got a Mexican nephew. Our family is growing. It already speaks four languages: Russian, Hebrew, English and Spanish. Dad creates, and I continue to sell his paintings. Many friends ask us, "How do you like Mexico?" It is a calm, quiet place where time has stopped. There is white sand, incredible blue sea, and the streets are filled with laughter and Mariachi music.

I've driven my daughter to school. Whose idea was it to start school at seven in the morning? I've greeted equally dozy teachers and parents like me. Now I'm going back home. A little exercise, and then "Good morning!" to the office. After all, today is my family's anniversary. It's been exactly 30 years since we left the Soviet Union. How much has changed! But the most important thing is that we are together, the family is growing, and Dad continues to create. Before entering the office, I need to take a sedative, but I'd rather do breathing exercises. Of the more than 50 employees, I arrived first.

Our office is a green building separated from our homes. Father has designed it himself; it's over 8,600 square feet—a gigantic mansion! The Russian word for "Studio" is written in white letters on the facade. This is an improvisation of our architect: he wanted to surprise us and took the word from Google translator. Unfortunately, that wasn't the most reliable translator and he initially wrote "Mausoleum." With great difficulty, we were able to detach these letters and replace them with the more or less appropriate word "Studio." The ground floor is divided into two parts: in one employees stretch canvases on stretchers, in the second they package and ship paintings, all of which is directed by Freddy.

I go up to the second floor. Here is the heart of the company—marketing and legal department. I hear someone running behind me. It is Gera; he leads the department of secondary sites. Gera is a tall, thin guy, about 26 years old; his arms are covered with tattoos, his eyes are always red, but you never know if it's because he's overworked or because he's spend the night in a club. His face somehow reminds me of the actor Ethan Hawke. Gera has been with us for more than five years; he is the most reliable employee, but not in terms of work.

Apart from our store at afremov.com, we operate on all existing Internet platforms in the world, and those are in five languages. Gera directs this department, which is responsible for all these websites. After Gera gets here, Olga comes in. She is a pretty blonde, and very responsible and hardworking. She cares about the department, which deals with social networks. Now I am going to my office which is getting equipped with a studio for live broadcasts. The plans is that once a day I will speak to our friends on Facebook, giving them the opportunity to watch my father as he paints. Then there are our lawyers' offices, the Franchising Department and at the very end there is the office of my brother Boris. Once upon a time he was small and skinny, then cheerful and reckless, and now he is a respectable and well-padded man who leads all this mess. As for me, I supervise only the Sales Department as I always have.

Sometimes I offer fresh ideas so that no one gets bored. I am going up to the third floor and see a huge poster over the stairs: "No entry for unauthorized people. Violators will be dismissed." I open the door with a combination lock and get into my dad's studio. He does not like to be disturbed. He and his students work there. Together they make copies; before lunch father creates originals, then finishes copies.

The students make a pencil drawing, paint the background, put in a lot of strokes, and then father finishes the picture, so it is not very different from the original. Of course, it would be nice if they painted everything themselves, but dad would never sign a picture that has not been finished by him. But with whom is he having such a lively conversation? It is our friend, also an artist, named Dima, and he lives in a nearby town. The subject of their discussion is, obviously, art.

"Lyonya, listen, what you sell is not art—it's just copies of your own works."

Father responds. "Art, in my opinion, does not exist. There is a skill, there is a craft, and those who do not own them, cannot claim to create great things. And there is a widespread opinion that 30% of paintings in the museums of the world are fakes. They are not the fakes produced by some malicious criminals. They are fakes made by the artists of the paintings themselves. It happens like this: an artist achieves fame and recognition, his paintings are quickly bought out, and he simply cannot cope with orders any longer. Then he gathers a group of students who help him. Look, would we know much about the artist Verocchio, if his young student Leonardo da Vinci had not painted an angel on his picture? Students always help their masters. I have been in the house museum of Rembrandt in Amsterdam, and there are pictures of his students hanging there, which don't look any different from Rembrant's paintings. So who really knows if it is his own paintings in the museums or one of his student's? I remember a film about the artist El Greco. He worked in Titian's workshop. And here unfolds a scene: the old maestro Titian is moving around a huge workshop filled with canvases, behind which his students are sitting, he gives instructions and tells to the young El Greco: "If you don't do it as I say, I will not sign this picture." He limits himself to telling others what to do, then signs the paintings. Nothing but that signature binds him to the painting. There are many similar stories in museums and the art market. This is what I call the artists' fakes; by the way, even the late Impressionists did a little of that. I wondered for a long time why, for example, some Renoir paintings look like merely painted canvas, and some of them are real masterpieces. I've decided not to follow the beaten path: I paint each original myself from beginning to end, and my students make copies of these originals. I don't try to hide it. I openly admit that and the price of such copies is 10-20 times less than of those pictures that I've painted myself."

"But still you finish all these pictures."

"Who cares, the main thing is that I'm perfecting my technique. Look at these new originals. Even I cannot repeat them, they are unique."

I don't like to get involved in such disputes. To my mind, art is what is painted from the heart, and it does not matter whether it is a copy or an original. I'd better go down, yell at Gera, provide support and guidance to Olga, sit at my desk, look through the window and remember the words of my mother: "It will not always be so." And Father's words in response: "Everything will keep getting better."

Printed in Great Britain
by Amazon